CONFESSIONS
of a Money Rock Star

How to shift from debt & despair to wealthy & worry free

MICHELLE COOPER
STOKE Publishing

Copyright 2017 © Michelle Cooper. All rights reserved.

Copyright fuels creativity encourages diverse voices, promotes free speech and creates a vibrant culture. Thank you for buying an authorized edition of this book and for complying with copyright laws by not reproducing, scanning or distributing any part of it in any form without permission. You are supporting the writer and allowing her to continue to publish works which may impact our world.

This book is available at special quantity discounts for bulk purchases, special events and educational purposes.

For details, write: michelle@michellebcooper.com
ISBN: 978-1-988675-09-1

Published in Canada

Foreword

Close your eyes and picture the successful modern woman. What do you envision?

For some, the successful modern woman is at the top of the corporate ladder. For others, she is managing a business she's created from the ground-up. Maybe she is traveling the world. Maybe she is an activist in her hometown. Maybe she has kids. Maybe she doesn't.

But one thing universal in all of these definitions of success--the modern woman has it all: fantastic health, thriving relationships, life clarity, remarkable talent, an almost intangible combination of grace and grit. She's created a lifestyle fueled by the ability to burn through cash as she wants, on what she wants, while staying in financial integrity.

She's not in debt. She either earns more than she spends or has access to funds that support her life in total abundance.

With definitions of achievement tied directly to earning and spending potential, not only can it feel overwhelming to figure out what you want to do, but once you do know your goals executing them can feel even more daunting-- especially when it comes to making and managing our own money.

Can you relate?

As modern women with ambitions for our own lives, careers, businesses, health, it's time to rethink our relationships to what society has been telling us all along-- especially as it relates to our financial health.

Like a cinder block tied to our back, if we don't learn to how to manage it intelligently it may just make it impossible to swim, pushing us to bottom of the deep end. It doesn't have to feel like this though. Creating a positive and peaceful relationship with money is possible. But how? Through earning more? Budgeting? By forgoing unnecessary luxuries like lattes and handbags?

Striving for higher earnings, more savings, and long-term financial plans that leave behind a legacy of abundance for those we love will advance our economic lives if we play our cards correctly, but even that will leave us feeling listless and burnt if we don't dive a bit deeper first! While paying attention to how much we earn, spend, invest and save is non-negotiable when it comes to rewriting our money story, and ultimately having a more peaceful relationship with our finances, it's not exclusively the answer either.

We need a more comprehensive solution.

We need to examine a spiritual association with money in order to get off the hedonic treadmill--the treadmill that tells us we have to earn more, to spend more, to prove our worth and value to others; that we have to compete with others to earn our keep. You see earning more, and simultaneously needing more, doesn't leave any space for peace.

Why bother to strive in the first place if contentment isn't a part of the end-game?

To arrive at contentment (and abundance), we must undo a paradigm that tells us that not only are we not good with money, but we are also undeserving of it. And no matter how much we earn, we'll always need more.

In the words of feminist theologian Meggan Watterson, "we don't earn our worth, we claim it." Inherent in our indwelling divinity lies an ever-flowing source of abundance and worthiness—our soul. In modern times, where we've been trained to commodify our time and talent to earn money, this inherent worthiness gets lost in the ongoing need to prove ourselves again and again. On the treadmill of earning our worth, we run to the beat of "I am not good enough," a beat that can drive us into the ground if we let it. But underneath this impulse of shame-based ambition exists an eternal truth, the essence of our existence. A thread of worthiness that isn't earned, it's retrieved. It's uncovered and it's claimed.

Getting to this place of self-acceptance, self-love and real-world abundance, often requires slaying years of conditioning that has told us that our value comes in the forms of meeting other people's needs, by emphasizing our physical beauty, conforming to other people's standards and expectations.

As Michelle expertly points out in the book, becoming a money rock star requires undoing shame. It requires processing the fears, limiting beliefs, family stories that tell you that you have to earn your worth and prove your value (again and again) to keep your head above water. It requires work, but not any work, the right kind of work—the type of work that takes you on a journey through your interior world to reclaim your inherent essence of worth within. In doing so, your external world becomes much clearer, and brighter.

I encourage you to embrace to this book as a journey. A journey to unleashing your inherent holiness and eternal worth as a precious step on the journey of rewriting a distorted relationship to money and wealth. Afterall, what do you have to lose anyway?

Jennifer Racioppi
Chart Your Success
www.jenniferracioppi.com

Dedication

This book is dedicated to my higher power, The Universe, my inner cosmos and my intuition – I have all I need inside me. It is dedicated to the gifts I have been given, that didn't feel like gifts at the time. They felt like fucking struggles. I see clearly now!

This book is also dedicated to Holly, Ostara, and Tyr – my children, who laugh with me, and at me, as I move through change and experience new things. I'm grateful for their souls and love their energy.

I'm grateful.

"What you seek is seeking you." - Rumi

My Confessions

If you have picked up this book, you want more money. Bam. There it is. I said it. If there is anything you need to know about me, it's that I say it like it is. I keep it real. Most of us want more – more money, more love, and more success. And all of that is often seen as ABUNDANCE. But I am going to challenge you to rethink that a little – to shift your thinking and thus shift your life. But first, let me share a little secret.

I have not always been a "money rockstar" – in fact, I have been a money deadbeat. I have been a money mess – not knowing what to do, where to turn, how to do it, and often asking myself if it was even worth trying to fix? Money is related to our emotions. It conjures feelings of joy and excitement but it also, quite frequently conjures feelings of not enough, of failure or desperation and of despondence – what is the point in all of this? I'll never get out of this mess. This is a hopeless situation.

I have been there. I have sat in those feelings and thought, I'll never get out. I have borrowed money I couldn't repay – and then tried to avoid repaying it with a plethora of excuses. I have racked up credit card debt, repeatedly. Yes, you read that right – REPEATEDLY. All those people who tell you to cut up the card, freeze it in a block of ice, or close the account. – yeah, those people – maybe they were right, but I didn't listen to them. And, let's get real here, in the world we live in, you need at least one credit card if you ever want to go anywhere or do anything. Ever try checking into a hotel without a credit card? Renting a car, or even a freaking bike? How about trying to operate a business, with recurring payments for software? Nope, not even possible.

I've also read ALL the books. The next book was the "fixer" – oh this time, it will be different. This person will be able to fix me. How did that work out? Well, I learned a lot. I learned what didn't work for me, what maybe would work for me if I had "the willpower" and eventually, what did work for me – and it didn't come from one book. It was a compilation of learning, information, personal development, spiritual connection, trust, clarity, and courage. So, yes, I've made mistakes. I've done things wrong. But I've learned some things along the way that I am going to share with you and if you do these things, you will experience abundance. That's a pretty big claim, I know. But I've done it, so I know it works. And I didn't pay a gazillion dollars for someone to teach it to me. I didn't get paid by someone else to regurgitate this message. This is how I came to change my relationship with money and therefore, the wealth in my life.

About Your Journey

The journey. No, not the band, even though I happen to love Journey. Don't Stop… Believing! I know you're not here to listen to me sing, though. You are here to begin your journey into wealth, into abundance and into all the money the Universe has to offer you, so let's get started!

As you are a going to be money rock star too, this is what we're going to call your "Rock Star Tour of Abundance." Think of yourself as a rock star embarking on their next world tour, and just like them, you need to prepare. Well, hold the bus because you're coming along on this tour! You might be asking yourself, "Do I really want to go on this journey with you?"- or maybe even screaming it. Let me answer that for you; if you're tired of repeating the same cycle like a broken record, your broke ass forever trapped in Crapville, then YES, you absolutely want to go on this journey with me. So get on the bus, cause we are hitting the road to abundance.

Your Rock Star Tour is awesome; it's lavish and we are making it rain 24/7. Don't you think it's about time for you to make a change for you? In life, we can get stuck. We can get stuck in relationships we shouldn't be in anymore. We can get stuck in jobs we have outgrown. We can get stuck in behaviors and habits that do not serve us. We can get stuck in boring towns full of stupid people. And, most importantly, we can get stuck in the cycle of scarcity and monetary lack that we placed ourselves into because we didn't know any better.

I say SCREW THAT CRAP.

Together, let's grow, let's expand, let's change, let's shift and let's evolve.   Let's rock this! In this journal, we're going to accomplish a lot. We are going to get to the root story of your scarcity and lack, the foundations of your money objections and we will discover how your experiences have formed your financial decision-making. We are going to examine your money-core values, practice self-responsibility and forgiveness and most importantly, we are going to journal OUR way to wealth. This is a process. It has been proven to work, and if you're committed to it, you will build your wealth.

It's really that simple.

As we embark on our journey to change, shift and evolve, we owe it to ourselves to step into our power. Together, let's change the things that are not serving us, not working for us, and that which is sabotaging us from facing our fears.

You see in life, we learn through experience. We learn that when the stove is hot, don't touch it or you will get burned, and that hurts. We learn that sometimes we think we are rocking our lives, and other times we are simply NOT – we are sucking the big banana. Often, it all leads back to one thing that time and again creeps into the picture- SHAME.

Brené Brown, the world-renowned shame, and vulnerability researcher says "Shame, for women, is this web of unobtainable, conflicting, competing for expectations about who we're supposed to be. And it's a straight-jacket." I would add - a straight-jacket that keeps money from you and traps you in a cycle scarcity, lack, and fear.

I love to personify shame because then I can see it right when it shows up. If you consider yourself to be the rock stars that you are, you know there are always "trolls," just waiting to latch onto your awesomeness and do whatever they can to ride your joy wave. You're familiar with that creepy guy or gal that attaches themselves to you like a tick, burying deep in your mind and tainting your thoughts – THAT is what shame is like. Most of us have experienced the "shame troll," as I like to call it - they want to buy you drinks, they stalk you on social media and oh! There they are again, hanging around, waiting to whisper some crap into your ear and derail all your awesomeness. Sometimes shame even disappears for a bit, recharging its batteries, but it will be back ready to rise and bitch slap you in the face! That metaphorical slap hurts, and more importantly sends you reeling into a spiral of your destructive habits. THAT is how I see shame and its path of destruction.

You may be thinking, "Oh, I just ignore that feeling," but ignoring it doesn't eradicate it. Ignoring it makes it more powerful. Ignored shame grows like the petri dish bacteria in your Grade 10 science class, but by uncovering it, digging into it – exposing it for what it is, we can begin to resolve it and shrink it. By shifting our thought patterns, focusing on the abundance we have, want and that which is yet to arrive, we become a little more shame-free each day. By amplifying the abundance that is your natural way of being when connected to your spiritual source and not living in shame we change our lives.

Confession:

When I began my business, I got very caught up in what everyone else was doing and how they were doing it. This online business world intrigued me but also overwhelmed me.

Well, that was a huge invitation to the world to take advantage of me. As I didn't know any better, when someone offered to help me take my business "online", I jumped at the chance! "The Six Figure Launch", "The 7 Figure Business Model", "The Laptop Lifestyle" - yup, that sounded freaking awesome and I was all in. I jumped in, feet first, and spent a big chunk of cash on someone who wasn't worth a dime. A con-woman who took my money and didn't give me one useful thing, let alone, solve my business issues.

So there I was, I had made a bad decision and I did my best to cover it up - to make it look like I'd never do something like that. I'm smart, right? I'm the money lady! Well, the shame of that situation became unbearable. It was like a giant troll that followed me around everywhere. Finally, I learned that I had to face up to what happened, my role, and how it all went down. And I had to forgive myself. It took a long time, but now I can laugh at it and it helps me understand other's bad financial decisions.

One thing has emerged crystal clear in my mind; if we don't get to the root of the shame that is affecting the majority of women in our world, they will never allow themselves to be successful nor can they create their legacy. And that would not be good for our world.

Sure, the short-term financial gain is achievable by utilizing strategies such as budgeting. Long-term financial security, however, will remain aloof until we go into the storm headfirst, getting to the root cause and looking shame in the face to say, "I fucking love and accept myself!" I won't lie, it can be uncomfortable, and it can feel like hard work, but together that is what we are here to do. Good people with money will change our world, and quite frankly, our world could do with a little changing – in fact, it's shifting right now, right in front of us, and if you are not onboard with it, you will remain poor. No one wants that! I sure don't.

The very first thing we should do is become honest with ourselves. We all lie to ourselves from time to time, or more than that if you're like me. I could lie to myself all day, every day if I allow it. I can tell myself a multitude of lies each day, but in the end, I just remind myself that I'm a rock star and that lie will affect me eventually, like an overdose at 3 a.m. in a seedy hotel. Now is not the time to lie to yourself. Now is the time to get real, get raw and get naked about your money. Write like no one will ever read a single word you're going to put down in ink. You can burn this book after if you want, but whatever you do, don't lie to yourself. Trust yourself. Trust the process. Surrender to the journey. You got this.

You are a rock star, just like me! In some areas of your life, you rock it out HARD in big ways, but in other areas maybe you sit in the shadows, watching, waiting and planning. When we find ourselves delaying or distracted from the commitment to our abundance, we are in the shadows. When we find ourselves consistently in "planning mode," we are in the shadows. When we find ourselves watching others, in comparison and judgment, we are in the shadows. When we find ourselves operating on the surface of our life, our journey and our commitment to our money, yup, you guessed it, we are in the shadows. Hanging out in the shadows is like hanging out in the wings of the rock star's stage – you can see it, you know it's there, the crowd is chanting for you, but you just don't take that step into the spotlight.

In this journal, we're going to shift that energy towards something positive, because once you rock out to your money, amplify your thoughts and actions, and make a commitment to continually practice abundance, life changes, my rock star friend. Once you break the cycle of scarcity and lack and hit the money playlist, your life will never be the same. Here we go, working through it together like the rock stars we are, traveling through our rock star tour of money, rocking out, rocking hard, owning our shit and killing it!

This is your Rock Star Tour of Abundance, so get to the bus — we are ready to hit the road!

"Surrender to what is. Let go of what was. Have faith in what will be." - Sonia Ricotti

Pardon The Interruption, I'm a Rock Star

We interrupt this show for an important message… you and your money!

Right now, you're probably stuck on some level of what I call the cycle of scarcity and lack- the story you keep telling yourself about money – how much you have- or don't have-, how it comes to you, where it comes from, and all the excuses and reasons you are in the place you are in. The cycle of scarcity and lack often forms the basis of our lives without us even realizing it. We are going to put a giant stick in that wheel, halt that thinking and start moving into wealth right now.

The interruption of that cycle is key to breaking these habitual ways of thinking in order to create new ways of living. Whether you are new to these concepts or deep within them, you may still be in the cycle and not realize it. Think of it like a new world tour to never before explored cities with your band. When you're stale, you suck. Period.

Sucking sucks and no one wants to suck! We all know that. Habits are just things we do when in default-mode because they're easy. Easy feels good, so good, but if we want more money, we need to change some habits. Maybe it doesn't feel so easy at first, but it will one day, I promise you. It's sort of like doing crunches – they suck, and when you don't have any abs, they suck even more. After you have done a bunch and built up some muscle, though, they become easier. They may remain challenging, but gradually the challenge is reduced. You just have to keep at them in order to maintain that washboard stomach!

Right now, we are going to shake things up and interrupt the cycle of scarcity and lack with exploration. When we are living in the cycle, we may become paralyzed by fear and do nothing, or just continue to do what we have done. Why? Because it's easier than changing our path. This is destructive to our abundance, so we are going to tackle this head on, moving straight into the eye of the storm. When we face things head on especially- when they feel uncomfortable, we achieve incredible momentum and progress.

What's the Story, Morning Glory?

The cycle starts with the story.

Are you asking "what story?" You know, that story that you keep telling yourself? It goes a little something like this…

I never have any money.
I am not good with money.
Must be nice to be her, with all that money.
I'm an idiot with money.
Money confuses me.
I don't like dealing with all that money stuff.
In order to make money, I have to work really hard and that sucks.
I want to hang out at the beach.
I'll never have any money; I'm an artist/creative/spiritualist.
I always lose money. As soon as I get money, it's gone.
I don't know where all my money goes!
If I have money, someone will take it away from me.
If I have money, my friends won't like me.
Money gives me anxiety.
Rich people are greedy and evil.
I'll never get out of debt.

The above statements are just some of the core stories that you may be telling yourself about money. There are so many of them, and we make up new ones all the time. If there's one thing we're good at, it's this habit. These stories originate from scarcity and lack of having. They come from your mindset and your beliefs that money is limited, there's not enough to go around, and that it is a commodity that we need to grab when it comes our way and hoard it under the stairs in case the crazy tax man comes calling. There's fear, there's scarcity and there's lack.

Confession:

As fast as I make money, it goes. I am always playing catch up. Throughout my life, I have been able to make or receive great sums of money, however, it always goes somewhere.

A debt pops up that I didn't deal with. I inherited some money when my dad died. I loaned a bunch of it out and then wham – suddenly I got a call from the student loan people who I had "forgot" all about.

How did they even find me, I was living in another country? There goes the rest of the money.

My underlying belief was that as fast as money comes to me, it goes so why even bother, I'll always be in the negative.

What statements above do you identify with?

What is the core story you have created about money? By discovering your core story – your generational and inherited money language, along with your early experiences of money- you are free to uncover the giant mountain in the way of your Rock Star Tour – the root shame story. Remember when we talked about that earlier? Shame. The shame troll that whispers in your ear, making you doubt yourself, keeping you small and in a cycle of crappy habits that destroy any abundance you even try to generate.

The tour bus cannot get around this obstacle – the giant mountain of shame. It can't get over it or get under it. It has to drive right through it.

Are you ready to dive into your root story?

Right here, right now, just like Van Halen said back in the 80's! Take some time with these questions, as they form the very deep belief that you are carrying around about money that you may not even be aware of.

Journaling is like a love song to your soul, and it is a key strategy to interrupting the cycle, moving through it and beginning the healing process. Free writing (writing like no one is ever going to read what you write, with no structure required,) is a more effective way to uncover your story. It often comes in layers, just like a music festival – one act after another. Just when you think you have seen the headline act, there may be another act that is on another stage! Don't shy away from it. With each act or layer, you level up to new abundance.

Let's get started...

What do you remember your Mom saying about money?

_____
_____
_____
_____
_____
_____
_____
_____
_____
_____
_____
_____

What do you remember your Dad saying about money?

_____
_____
_____
_____
_____
_____
_____
_____
_____
_____
_____
_____

What was your family's experience with money? Did you have a lot, a little or maybe you didn't even know?

_____
_____
_____
_____
_____
_____
_____
_____
_____
_____
_____

What actions did you see your parents taking with money? Were they always handing money out, or did they keep it? Were you given an allowance for chores, or perhaps just an amount each week just because? Did bill collectors appear at your door? Was there bankruptcy? Did your family win the lottery?

_____
_____
_____
_____
_____
_____
_____
_____
_____
_____
_____

Is there an experience in your childhood that stands out about money?

_____
_____
_____
_____
_____
_____
_____
_____
_____
_____

What is your earliest memory of money? Did you make your own money with a lemonade stand or other entrepreneurial venture, or did you just receive money or demand it?

_____
_____
_____
_____
_____
_____
_____
_____
_____
_____
_____
_____
_____
_____
_____

What is the biggest financial mistake you have made? Are there lots of them? Can you see a pattern?

_____
_____
_____
_____
_____
_____
_____
_____
_____
_____
_____
_____

What is the biggest financial risk you have taken? What happened? Who was involved?

_____
_____
_____
_____
_____
_____
_____
_____
_____
_____
_____
_____

Did the risk pay off?

_____
_____
_____
_____
_____
_____
_____
_____

What do you feel embarrassed about in regards to your money? What is your deep, dark secret?

_____
_____
_____
_____
_____
_____
_____
_____
_____
_____
_____
_____

What do you feel ashamed of in regards to your money? Is there anything you hide e.g. price tags, receipts or transactions? Do you have a "secret" bank account or credit card?

Pulling the Stories Together

Now that we have uncovered a whole lot of stories, beliefs, traumas, opinions, and thoughts, we can pull them together. What comes to the surface are a few key stories and situations that we are holding on to with shame at the forefront of our minds. Here's a real-life example that may help you pull your shame story together.

> *Melody had always received money from her Dad. He gave it to her for being a "good girl," as he called her. What did being a "good girl" mean? It meant that she didn't make waves. She didn't cause a commotion. She went along, seen but not heard, with her role in her family as a dutiful daughter. Her mother, she witnessed, was given a "household allowance" – money to run the home and allocate how she wished. However, her dad had expectations – namely, that the home ran smoothly. If things were not smooth at home, the money stopped. Thus Melody learned at an early age that in order to have money, you could not cause a commotion. You had to just go with the flow. "Someone" would give you money if you did this. You were completely powerless in this situation – you had no control. Melody moved into adulthood, continually taking money from her dad. When he gave her money, he felt good and she felt good – like he was rescuing her. Of course, she couldn't manage money – that was someone else's role. She was the victim and money came from the rescuer. When Melody started to earn her own money, her body felt uncomfortable. Her nervous system felt on edge, and she unconsciously got rid of the money as soon as she could. Melody ended up in a ton of credit card debt that her dad repeatedly had to pay off for her. This fed his relationship with money as well as hers – it is now clear that it was a co-dependent relationship with money and if she ever wanted to live her dreams, she had to get out of this cycle.*

From all of the journaling you have done above, pull together your story. At the end, you will uncover your own deep, dark secret you hold about your money that you wouldn't want anyone, not a single person to know – that is the story that is holding you back from the rock star abundance that is yours, waiting for you to grab hold of it and live your dreams.

Your MoneyDate

By creating awareness and accountability around our money, we show it the attention it craves and deserves. We also create the energy that attracts more into our lives. Like the fans at your rock concert, your money wants your undivided attention at regular intervals – it needs it, or it will find another rock star to become obsessed with.

Your MoneyDate. It's exactly what it sounds like- your date with your money. This is the time that you devote to your money and the action steps that seal the deal in building your wealth. Having a weekly MoneyDate where you check the balances on all your accounts – banks, credit cards and online resources like PayPal, provides awareness. Make sure to check as well as how much is owed to you and how much you owe others. This is a great tool for accountability, but also an action step that builds your money rituals. Setting your priorities each week around your money will move you in a forward momentum and take control of where your money comes from and goes to, and it is empowering.

If your bestie called you and asked you for your time, would you put it off? Would you hesitate? I sure as heck wouldn't because my bestie is important to me. I'd get that time in my schedule NOW. And if they said, "Hey Rock Star, let's do this every week" it would become a non-negotiable date in my schedule. Make a commitment to your money and schedule that time – set aside one hour each week to hang out with your money. If possible, make it the same day and time each week, and make it non-negotiable- rain or shine, it happens. It is your date with your fan, your bestie, and your abundance.

When that date comes up, you need resources and access to information! Use a journal or *Your MoneyDate Journal,* which is a great resource for tracking your money and recording the progress each week. If you haven't already purchased *Your MoneyDate Journal*, pick one up as the date format is all set out for you.

You also need access to bank accounts, credit card accounts, your bookkeeping system, wherever you store all this awesome stuff. Don't plan to do your money date at the beach if you don't have access to the info you need on your phone. Set yourself up for success – a pretty journal where you record this information, a drink you enjoy, some awesome music playing – this is a date, right?

Money is part of a Universal cycle – it flows both to you and away from you, and you are not only a part of that cycle, you are a participant in it. Money flows to you, perhaps from different sources, perhaps at different times of the month, but it's always flowing to you. Money that you have or is owed to you is commonly referred to as your ASSETS. Yup, you have them. They may be big or small but you have them. We look at three main areas:

- Bank accounts
- Accounts Receivable – money owed to you (this could be business or personal loans)
- Other places you are holding money like Paypal, gift cards or prepaid cards.

Go through all your accounts and write out the balances – chequing, savings, PayPal.

Let's talk Accounts Receivable. This is the money that is owed to you for services you have provided in your business or money that is owed to you because you lent it out to someone. Maybe you lent money to your broke-ass brother – that's an account receivable as much as a client who you created a website for and hasn't yet paid you for. You can find this information in your bookkeeping software, or even better, ask your bookkeeper. However, I invite you to think about why people owe you money. How much is it? When are they going to pay you? How do you collect money from clients or your customers? Do you accept credit cards? If you don't, well you may as well be living in the dark ages. Get that money in your bank account – if your price can't absorb 2-3% processing fees, then you have bigger problems. Seek advice from a professional.

Take Action People! Action-Jackson Gets Shit Done! What are you going to do to collect money that is owed to you? What are your priorities for your money? Write this down.

Now, how do your assets make you feel? Write in your journal about this. Pause for a moment and sit with it. Close your eyes, and identify where in your body you feel this and what your body is telling you about the feeling. Journal, journal, journal!

The second half of the money cycle is money that flows away from you. In a healthy cycle, the money that flows away from you feels good! You receive a bill, you are grateful for the service or product that the bill provided and so you are ecstatic to pay that bill. Be ecstatic, be grateful, be in as high a vibration in the outflow of money as you are in the inflow of money. Sometimes we spend money we don't have yet, we borrow money or we use credit facilities to complete transactions. These are your LIABILITIES – the money you owe. This includes your:

- Credit cards
- Loans
- Accounts payable

Check all your credit card and loan balances. Write them down in detail. Note when payment is due.

What the heck are accounts payable, you may be asking? It is services or products that you have received, and now you have a bill for them, but you haven't yet paid for it. Let's say you owe money to someone – be that the electric company, your bookkeeper, or your friend who lent you $50 at the last home party you went to because you just had to have that thingy majig. That is an account payable. If you're in a business, you can get an accounts payable report from your bookkeeping software or your bookkeeper.

Remember Action Jackson? Here she comes again to take action. What are you going to do right now or in the next seven days to pay these liabilities? What money do you need to move around? What are some upcoming expenses that you should be budgeting for? Prepare ahead of time. When we don't prepare, we use our credit card and we are then in debt! Don't do that! Prepare for expenses.

And of course, we need to talk to ourselves about this – fortunately, we have that handy thing called journaling we've been practicing. How does your deadline date make you feel? How can you improve your situation? What are you grateful for in regards to money right now? Always seal this process with gratitude. Write out one thing you're grateful for and three reasons why.

Pursekeeping

What does your wallet look like? Would a pick-pocket give it back? Is it a rag-tag mess of receipts, cards and miscellaneous items? Do you have items in there that don't relate to money? Oops, I think there may be a cigarette in there from 20 years ago! When you open it, are you nervous about what may or may not fall out? Would CSI be able to identify you and where you have been by your wallet?

Your wallet's purpose is to hold your money. It's simple. It doesn't contain your phone, your passport or your stash. It contains your money and items associated with your money like your Citrine (more on that later!), your credit cards, your checkbook (yeah, they still make those things) and your bank cards. Cleaning out your wallet creates a sacred space for your money to live in and thrive. I'm not saying that you need to iron your dollar bills, well, maybe I am, but if that doesn't jive with you, that's okay. Just don't mix up your money with your crazy handbag where you keep all sorts of crap that you may just need on the tour.

The way you keep your money gives the Universe a sign as to whether or not you're ready for your fortune to multiply. Make sure your bills are neatly arranged in your wallet or it is in some kind of order. De-clutter it and get rid of the trash you no longer need such as receipts, etc. Reverence for your cash will go a long way. Your wallet should say something about you. What does yours say? Does it say that you're a homeless hobo living on the railroad, or does it say you are a rock star?

Maybe you need to invest in a rock star wallet – it could be one of the best investments for your future. So, if your wallet is a mess, change it up. If you don't have a wallet, buy one. Invest in a sacred vessel for your money.

What about your bank account? Can it accept money in different forms? By electronic means, credit card, bank machine, and just plain cash? Is there a limit to how much you can deposit? Here's a funny historical fact about money. Many years ago, when lotteries were just beginning, many accounts wouldn't allow the winners to deposit their winnings as they couldn't handle that amount of money. Of course, they fixed that, but every lottery winner is now provided with an optional advisor to help them "manage" the flow of money. Ask your bank for the deets – because a wave of money will soon be flowing to you.

Confession:

Wallet? What wallet?

For the longest time, my "wallet" was a make up bag that I got from one of those monthly subscription services. I liked the make up bag, but it wasn't a wallet. I had told myself that "wallets were for old people". Seriously!

One day, as I pulled out my make up bag in a store to pay for my purchase, I couldn't find my bank card. I had some change floating around and I started dumping the contents all over the cashier's desk. I felt like an idiot and a child - completely inept with her money. I thought to myself "this is ridiculous!" Right then I decided to buy the best wallet I could afford and since then, so many people comment on how beautiful it is. It makes me feel happy and proud of my money instead of stupid and disrespectful.

"Forgiveness is a gift you give yourself."
- Tony Robbins

Forgiveness

Now that we have identified some of our generationally inherited money stories and behaviors, as well as some financial mistakes, we can begin leaving them behind, in the past, where they belong. Forgiving yourself is the first step. Like the sacred 12-step programs that save many a rock star, this is your 12-step program, except there aren't 12 steps, there's only two: forgive and love yourself - save your soul, have more money.

The power of forgiveness is miraculous. Forgiveness is one of the strongest actions you can take to heal your shame and any trauma that is associated with it. It's continual; you may forgive yourself right now for something, but another thing will come up, or the first thing will come back in another form, or you will need to go deeper with that original brand of forgiveness. Remember our shame trolls? Well, they are sitting there, fighting the forgiveness that you so badly want to cultivate, trying to keep forgiveness off the tour like a jealous groupie. Be aware of that dynamic because it can derail your journey – in effect, it can halt your concert tour. Don't stop believing.

My forgiveness process originates in ho'oponopono, the ancient Hawaiian forgiveness practice. Many people have understood ho'oponopono to be a mantra where one repeats the words 'I'm sorry, please forgive me, thank you, I love you' as a form of mental and spiritual cleaning that could be compared to Buddhist techniques for clearing karma. It has been defined as a forgiveness and reconciliation practice, cleansing of 'errors of thought' – the origin of problems and sickness in the physical world, according to the Hawaiian culture. The literal translation is 'to put to right; to put in order or shape, correct, revise, adjust, amend, regulate, arrange, rectify, tidy up, make orderly or neat."

I invite you to try it specifically in relation to your situation or circumstances around money. It truly was a shifting moment in my move into abundance, and I advocate for this process strongly. So, let's get started, rock star! We can begin by forgiving ourselves for our money history – our past mistakes, bad judgment, the debt we built up, bankruptcy, theft, distrust, mismanagement of our cash and maybe just stories we have carried forward unconsciously. By forgiving ourselves, we begin to release the shame of our pasts. Forgiving ourselves can be work, it can take a while and it is a practice that may never go away, but it is key to your abundance.

I'm Sorry

Acknowledge that you created the pain, anxiety, stress or discomfort that you are experiencing around money. Acknowledge that you are responsible for the mistakes you made. You may have been unaware that you carried these memories or thoughts inside yourself. Now, you can take 100% responsibility for all of this.

I'm sorry for…

_____
_____
_____
_____
_____
_____
_____
_____
_____
_____
_____
_____
_____
_____
_____
_____
_____
_____
_____
_____
_____
_____

Forgive Me

You did not know that you held onto these thoughts or memories inside of you. Ask your inner rock star for assistance with your self-forgiveness. After all, you allowed these actions or memories to affect your present life and abundance.

Forgive me for…

_____
_____
_____
_____
_____
_____
_____
_____
_____
_____
_____
_____
_____
_____
_____
_____
_____
_____
_____
_____
_____
_____
_____

Thank You

Release and cleanse this memory by thanking it for appearing and providing the opportunity to free yourself from it. You can also thank your inner rock star for helping you with this liberation.

Thank you for…

_____
_____
_____
_____
_____
_____
_____
_____
_____
_____
_____
_____
_____
_____
_____
_____
_____
_____
_____
_____
_____

I Love You

You love and accept yourself just the way you are, in this exact place that you are in. Only love heals. You are speaking to both your memories and to yourself.

I love you ...

___

In the end, all that matters is that you can look at yourself and say…

I'm sorry
Forgive me
Thank you
I love you

Forgiveness is not a one-time event; it's continual. You should journal your forgiveness once a week. Work towards the goal of looking yourself in the mirror and saying I'm sorry, forgive me, thank you and I love you from your journaling points. When you can do this without any triggers, tears or doubt, you are in the forgiveness process and making progress. Don't give up. This is difficult, it could take you days, weeks or months to get to this point, but we want to continually work towards this point as it is salvation.

Confession:

I found self-forgiveness hard. Yup, there I said it. I was certainly not a rock star at forgiveness. I discovered that it was easier for me to forgive others than it was for me to forgive myself. I stood in front of a mirror many times, trying really hard to "do this." Fail. Fail. Fail. It took a long time for me to be able to forgive myself for past financial mistakes – because I felt like I made a lot of them. Like, A LOT. And forgiving myself meant owning up to my role, my actions and my weaknesses and failures. Looking at myself in the mirror and attempting the ho'oponopono was really difficult and as my eyes darted around the mirror, I found myself looking everywhere BUT in my own eyes. So just know that this may take a while and its impact is progressive.

"Be thankful for what you have; you'll end up having more. If you concentrate on what you don't have you will never, ever have enough."
- Oprah Winfrey

GRATEful Dead

Gratitude is a hot word in our world right now and there is a reason for that; it works. Seriously, it works. Gratitude is humbling, loving and empowering. It ignites the flow of money and we are divinely compensated for it.

Incorporating gratitude into your day brings more abundance to your life by raising your body's vibration and energetic frequency. You see, we all have an energetic signal that is sent out into the world like a vibration in a pool of water. Imagine dropping a rock into a clear pool of water – the vibration of the rock creates the ripple that extends out from it. You are the pool of water and your thoughts are the rock. When we up-level our vibration and energetic frequency utilizing gratitude, it's like turning up the volume on everything you are already doing – amplifying it.

Forgiveness can feel draining like we have turned on a tap that we can't turn off. Complimenting every forgiveness exercise with gratitude will help you return to a better mindset and continue the amplification process. It is essential to this process. Always seal forgiveness with gratitude – every single time. However, I recommend a daily gratitude instalment to really ramp up the amplification of your money.

Gratitude journaling can seem like an overwhelming commitment if you have never done it, but it really is easy to incorporate with today's technology. There are gratitude apps, journaling apps and voice to text apps as well as websites focusing solely on expressing gratitude. You can even use the old-fashioned pen and paper! I love an excuse to buy a new notebook and pen, so make this one special. You can do it in your car, on a walk, in meditation, at the gym, in the shower, in yoga, or before you go to sleep – anytime is gratitude time, just like Miller Time.

Try this simple exercise to get you started.

I am grateful for…

_____
_____
_____
_____
_____

Three reasons why I am grateful are…

Bam. You're done! Drop the mic. Rinse and repeat daily.

"When you make a choice, you change the future."
- Deepak Chopra

Your Money Alignment Statement

So far we have done some work towards abundance and money; some hard, some not so hard, but here is where we get our game on, bitches! We are now moving into playing an active role in our money and co-creating our abundance. Taking 100% responsibility, forgiving ourselves plus taking inspired action is the essence of owning your power! We now move into a power position with our money.

You know that money story you identified – that crappy thing that brings you down and keeps you broke? Well, we are going to bust that story up! Mama Said Knock You Out! – Oh LL Cool J…. Wise words, wise words.

We need to rewire our brain with a replacement story – this is our Money Alignment Statement. When we uncovered our current shame story, we identified what has been limiting us and holding us back. We uncovered the subconscious ideas and stories that we carried forward into our lives, which in turn resulted in us probably making some kind of financial mistake that we now regret. Well, we are actively forgiving ourselves and can now replace all of that with how we want to feel about money, how we consciously interact with money and how we intentionally handle money. You see, when we align with how we want to feel, instead of a number or a thing, we change our body's chemistry. We change how our body is reacting to even the idea of loads of money. Your Money Alignment Statement is your replacement story that changes how you feel about money, the energy you emit regarding money, your vibration around money and ultimately how much money you have in your bank account.

Your Money Core Values

To start creating our Money Alignment Statement, we first delve into our money core values. We need to discover what we are aligned with and how we want to show up with money. Money core values are foundational beliefs about money that anchor our lives. They are the non-negotiable aspects of how you want to feel about money.

What are words that you positively associate with money? Look at the list and circle ALL the words that you feel are important to you regarding money. Not in life in general, not in your business or relationship – specifically about MONEY.

Acceptance	Clear-mindedness	Accomplishment
Clever	Accuracy	Closeness
Achievement	Comfort	Commitment
Active	Compassion	Adaptability
Completion	Adoration	Composure
Adventure	Confidence	Affectionate
Conformity	Alertness	Altruism
Connection	Ambition	Conscious
Amusement	Consistency	Appreciation
Content	Attractive	Conviction
Cooperation	Awareness	Courage
Balance	Courtesy	Beauty
Creativity	Superior	Credibility
Belonging	Curiosity	Daring
Bliss	Decisiveness	Boldness
Deference	Brave	Delight
Brilliance	Dependable	Calm
Camaraderie	Desire	Dando
Determination	Capability	Devotion
Care	Dignity	Diligence
Challenge	Directness	Charity
Discipline	Charm	Discovery
Discretion	Diverse	Clarity
Dominance	Dreamy	Eagerness
Educated	Giving	Effective
Grace	Efficiency	Gratitude
Elation	Gregarious	Elegance
Growth	Empathy	Happy
Harmony	Energy	Enjoyment
Helpful	Entertaining	Enthusiasm
Honesty	Honour	Exhilaration
Hopeful	Hospitable	Expertise
Humility	Exploration	Imagination
Extravagance	Impactful	Exuberance
Independence	Fair	Inquisitiveness
Fame	Insightful	Inspiration
Fascination	Integrity	Fearlessness
Intuition	Flexible	Flow
Fluency	Joy	Focus
Fortitude	Kindness	Freedom
Frugality	Liberty	Fun
Love	Loyalty	Meticulous
Relaxation	Mindful	Reliable
Modest	Resilience	Motivation
Optimism	Satisfaction	Outrageous
Passion	Self-reliance	Sensitive
Perfection	Sensual	Serenity
Sharing	Significant	Playful

Now, write them out here in rows of three.

Now compare the first row. Is there one that has more weight to it? Cross off the other one or two in that row. Move down the rows, until you are left with five to seven words. On some rows, you may have none left. These are your larger Money Core Values. Write them out here.

_____
_____
_____
_____
_____
_____
_____
_____
_____
_____

If you had to pick three, what would they be? What are your top three?

_____
_____
_____
_____
_____
_____
_____
_____
_____

If you were to think of money as your best friend, who would they be? Who is money to you? Well, that bestie encompasses your three core values. This is your mental clarity about what money is to you. Let's create a sentence about what our money is by taking the three main Core Values and adding them to 'MONEY IS'. For example, MONEY IS CONSISTENT, IN-FLOW AND HONEST.

Money is...
_____
_____
_____
_____
_____
_____
_____
_____

What words do you associate with how you want to FEEL about money? From the list below, circle all the words that jump off the page at you in relation to how you want to **FEEL** about money.

Joyful	Tenderness	Cheerful
Sympathetic	Content	Adoration
Proud	Fondness	Satisfied
Receptive	Excited	Interested
Amused	Delighted	Elated
Shocked	Enthusiastic	Exhilarating
Optimistic	Elated	Amazed
Trusting	Delight	Calm
Relaxed	Interested	Intrigued
Hopeful	Absorbed	Pleased
Curious	Confident	Anticipating
Brave	Eager	Comfortable
Safe	Happy	Loving
Lustful	Aroused	Tender
Compassionate	Caring	Infatuated
Trust	Attraction	Energized

Write them down here:

Just like you did last time, compare the first three. Is there one that has more weight to it? Cross off the other two in that row. Move through the rows, until you are left with three to five words. If you had to pick three, what would they be? What are your top three feelings that you want to have about money?

_____
_____
_____
_____
_____
_____
_____

Why is money in your life? Yeah, yeah, we know, so that you can eat, travel and pay the bills, but let's switch that up again. What if money is in your life so that you can feel certain emotions – great emotions that drive you to abundance? This is your emotional clarity about how you want to feel about money. We create this sentence by using the top three feeling words along with 'Money makes me feel.' For example, MONEY MAKES ME FEEL EXCITED, CURIOUS AND CALM.

Money makes me feel…
_____
_____
_____
_____
_____
_____
_____

Shared experience – if your money is your bestie, what do you and money experience together? This is your physical clarity around money. What do you want to experience physically in your wealth? We will create this sentence by knowing specifically how much money you want in the immediate future, what physical things you want and the experiences you desire. It could be a bank balance, an annual salary, a revenue target or some other amount that is important to you right now – not in the next ten years – right now, in the next one to six months. Be specific. Example, AS A RESULT, I HAVE $10,000 IN MY SAVINGS ACCOUNT AND NO DEBT.

As a result, I…

_____
_____
_____
_____
_____
_____
_____
_____
_____
_____
_____
_____
_____
_____
_____
_____
_____
_____
_____
_____

Commitment – oh that word, it makes many of us shrink! I'm sorry, but your bestie needs commitment. You must be committed to money if you want more of it. You must be committed to creating it and being an active partner with it. You must commit to the process. What are you committed to creating? This is the intention you are setting to create the money that you want. This is your action step. We create this sentence by deciding what you are going to do to stay in alignment with your money, with your core values, and with your feelings. This could be checking in on your bank balance, tracking your income and expenses, listening to podcasts, reading books and articles, getting further money education, inspiration or guided abundance meditations – all activities that support your intentions. For example, I AM COMMITTED TO MY DAILY MEDITATIONS, LEARNING, AND JOURNALLING.

I am committed to…

_____
_____
_____
_____
_____
_____
_____
_____
_____
_____
_____
_____
_____
_____
_____

Now we can bring all of these statements together into a beautiful money mantra – your **Money Alignment Statement.**

Money is _____, _____ and _____, and so I feel _____, _____, and _____.
As a result, I am/have _____ and I am committed to _____
_____

Now write out your Money Alignment Statement.
_____
_____
_____
_____
_____
_____
_____
_____
_____
_____
_____
_____
_____
_____
_____
_____
_____
_____
_____
_____

By creating your Money Alignment statement, you create and integrate a new emotion around money that fuels the life that you are striving for – your Rock Star Tour of Abundance! This is like the set list for your tour, so be in alignment with it.

Your money is attracted to your vibration and your energy, and your vibration is generated by your emotions. There is no result without action, so the more you align your actions with your money, the more money you will attract – you are co-creating this. When we clear the path, we clear the way for the natural flow of money to your life. The money is there, you just need to clear the pathway. Your alignment and this practice will generate new avenues for money to flow to you – it will find you, like your bestie at a crazy party!

Aligning your business or your job with your money and your emotions will attract more money. Share your alignment with your friends, family, and community and assert your money alignment into the world. Print your Money Alignment Statement and post it on your wall, write it on your mirror, on your social media feed, write it in your journal every day, say it as your meditation mantra. The more you interact with it, the more powerful it becomes. Tell people about your Money Alignment Statement. Share with them how you feel about money and even be willing to redirect them in their own negative language around money.

The next time some joker says to you, "Oh, I'm so broke!" perhaps challenge them to reframe that sentence or even assert your alignment by stating that you don't like to be around that type of language. Claiming your alignment and declaring it to the world amplifies your abundance. These actions will help you maintain your alignment and achieve your goals.

The more money I make, the bigger impact I make.

Confession:
I was having coffee with a friend at a great little café in our neighborhood. I was telling her about a show I saw about living and working abroad.

This is something I had done in the past and was considering doing again. I started telling her about my "plan". Her response was all about how that was nice and possible for me, but not her. She started telling me how she never has money to do this thing she wants. All the "I'm broke" language started flowing. It was uncomfortable to tell her that I couldn't be around that kind of language. She was taken aback so I explained the reasoning.

She didn't get it, and so the next time she asked if I wanted to go for a coffee, I said no. That may sound crazy and really mean, but when you are building your abundance, you need to be very particular about what you do, who you spend time with and the words that are used.

"Take a chance. It's the best way to test yourself. Have fun and push boundaries."
-Richard Branson

Rock Star Roadie Kit

Your Rock Star Roadie Kit supports your abundance – it's all the practices, the secrets, the tips, and tricks – all that magical stuff you do with, in and around your money. Some refer to this as "Stacking The Deck." What the heck does that mean, you ask? The literal definition of "stack the deck" means to adjust something so that the desired outcome is achieved. I say it means that you are putting yourself at an advantage. It means using all the 'extra' things that you feel aligned with that support your wealthy lifestyle. These are the things that put you at an advantage, like the rock star you are.

Some ways to stack the deck are the use of crystals, essential oils, meditation, reiki, astrology, and tarot… only you know what speaks to you! There are so many practices that you can use to stack the deck in your favor to achieve the wealth that you desire. The following are suggestions, but they aren't my advice or detailed instructions. If one of them pulls you in, I invite you to go further in your research and learning. I encourage you to keep an open mind with this and take inspiration from what speaks to you. Follow your intuition. Remember, your life is a rock star tour and so sometimes it goes into the unknown, like Jim Morrison walking through the desert – break on through. Explore, experiment, invite and have fun.

Abundance Visioning

An additional aspect of the replacement story is your abundance vision – what you see your life looking and feeling like when you are living with your money alignment. Abundance visioning exercises may include guided meditations, journaling and vision boards where you are able to step into your vision of abundance.

Guided visioning meditations allow your mind to go on a journey. Relax and enjoy the trip. Really lean into this process and see what comes up. The benefits of meditation are scientifically proven and becoming more and more mainstream. There are many meditation apps, websites and physical locations if that's your thing. There are three **guided visioning meditations** available in the bonuses at the back of the book to get you started. It is always beneficial to journal following a guided visioning meditation. Consider writing about what you saw, experienced, who was there with you, how you felt – as much detail as possible.

Abundance visioning may also include journaling exercises, where you spend time writing about your wealthy future. Further, in this book, we have journal prompts in our 30 Days of Money section. Journaling your vision can be incredibly powerful and you are encouraged to free write about your vision of your money future. Remember, this means to write like no one will read it! Once you have worked through those 30 days, consider repeating it, as your answers may change and evolve.

Vision boards are fun to create and a reminder of what we are declaring to the Universe is important to us! Creating a vision board can be as easy as gathering some magazines, cutting out pictures of what you want and pasting them onto a board. Place the vision board somewhere that you will see it – not in your closet. Or, you can go a different route with your board. Technology is our friend and an app like Pinterest is great for creating a vision board – it basically is a whole bunch of vision boards!

By incorporating abundance visioning exercises into our lives, we continually build our abundance muscles and move into our divine truth – our full expression of abundance and our natural right to all the money that we need. Spending time envisioning what the future looks like because you are living in alignment with your money is a key step to manifesting it into your reality. Envisioning yourself in your future attracts the energy that will make that future happen.

Meditation

Meditation in its truest form allows you to connect to your higher source – the Universe, the Cosmos, God. It is a great practice to cultivate more peace and happiness in life, as well as money! Who doesn't want that? Meditation isn't just for the super spiritual or the yoga culture, it is for everyone and especially for those who are trying to attract 'more' into their lives- those who are amplifying. As humans, we are either in one of two states – either our mind is running us, or we are running our mind. Meditation lets us press pause for a moment.

This is not a book to teach you how to meditate, but it's great to have an overview of how meditation works its wonders. Here comes the science – yup, here we are in Grade 10 Science class again. Stay with me here for a bit. There are five major categories of brain waves, each corresponding to different activities we do. Meditation enables us to move from higher frequency brain waves to lower frequency and calm the mind. Slower wavelengths equal more time between thoughts, which equals more opportunity to skilfully choose which thoughts you invest in. That is the simplest way I have come to explain meditation.

The Elixir of Abundance

Essential oils have been used in aromatherapy for thousands of years to attract riches and wealth for one's body, mind, spirit, and emotions. They are the lifeblood of plants and contribute to our well-being in so many ways – ways we can't even imagine!

These oils can be used either alone or in a blend with other oils to enhance their results and increase your attraction for wealth. Historically, oil blends have been inherited through family lineage as a way to pass on and continue a family's wealth. Often, we've heard tales of a Viking King passing his goats, chickens, thieved gold and magical potions onto his sons and daughters moments before he departs for battle – yeah, that kind of inheritance. Many of the oils in this list are considered "Holy" oils and have been used in traditional sacred healing rituals and ceremonial rites of passage. I say, bring on the ritual!

Many of the oils associated with prosperity are spice oils, which are known for their strong curative properties. In the days of the Silk Road, spice oils from the Orient were traded as valuable commodities on the world market and some were considered more valuable than gold.

If you're not convinced, here's some more science. Essential oils work on all four levels of your being – the physical, emotional, mental and spiritual. The application of the oil is like a magnet for money. They magnetize the electromagnetic energy field for attracting money and elevating your vibration to bring money to your life.

Great oils of money are:

- Cinnamon bark or leaf
- Myrrh Spikenard
- Sandalwood
- Ginger
- Patchouli

- Wild Orange
- Bergamot
- Galbanum
- Frankincense
- Clove

You can enhance your money vibration by using essential oils either aromatically or topically. Dispense 1-3 drops of one of the above oils or a blend that resonates with you into your palm, rub them together, close your eyes and begin to inhale. No, we aren't huffing glue here, we are inhaling the essence of abundance. Breathe deeply and allow yourself to relax. Say your Money Alignment Statement out loud, with confidence and clear intention. Lean into the feelings that are in your Money Alignment Statement – really feel those feelings. All the feelings, all the time.

You can also diffuse the oils. Diffusion is one of the simplest methods for using essential oils aromatically. You can purchase a diffuser pretty much anywhere these days, or you can simply have oil in a dish with water- it's as simple as that.

Topical application is a very effective method for applying essential oils because they easily penetrate the skin. Using a carrier oil (like fractionated coconut oil) can also increase absorption, especially in the skin that is dry, as it helps moisturize and slow the evaporation of the oil. In addition to putting the oils directly onto your skin, you could add oil to a warm bath or add it to a lotion that you already use. A word of caution, as the use of essential oils increases, so does the production of synthetic oils. Always check that your oils are 100% naturally, ethically sourced.

Crystals

Crystals may feel like a secret source of power – like magic. Or they may just feel like rocks, rumbling around in your pocket. The effectiveness of them is in the energy they hold and harness, and that energy has an effect on your overall vibration. Crystals have been used for many purposes throughout history and some relate more to money than others. Here are 10 crystals that will support your money alignment.

1. Green Aventurine: This is known as the "Stone of Opportunity" and is considered to be the luckiest of all crystals. It has great energy for attracting wins of any kind. Try carrying the stone with you all the time. A creative way to use Green Aventurine is to place it in your wallet or a loose change purse or jar.

2. Citrine: This is known as the "Merchant's Stone". Citrine attracts money like a magnet. Carry it with you, have it on your desk or, if you have a store, put it in your cash register.

3. Malachite: This is the stone of improvement. It is a great stone to carry with you when making financials deals or interviewing for a job that you really want. It can also help you in gaining prosperity by protecting you from attracting unreliable and dishonest people along with attracting righteous and helpful people for you.

4. Jade: In some cultures, this is considered THE stone for luck and prosperity. You can also change your luck by putting a small piece of this stone where you put your wallet or purse at night or where you put change at your business.

5. Pyrite: This stone is also known as Fool's Gold because it resembles gold to the untrained eye. It helps in making better decisions and helps you in spending your saved money wisely.

6. Peridot Gemstone: At a glance, this medium green crystal looks like a green colored emerald. According to experts, it represents ancestral money and affluence. If you are struggling with debt, then it is the best stone for you.

7. Ruby: This gemstone is great for people who desire to attract love along with prosperity. For this reason, gamblers usually keep this stone with them while playing on gambling tables to enhance their luck. You can also use this crystal to get right vibrations while attracting your love or luck in money matters.

8. Quartz or Smoky Quartz: This stone is fantastic for improving your overall luck. Spending money that has been charged with Quartz may attract more money. To charge the money, simply place the quartz on some of your money bills and set them in sunlight for few hours.

9. Tiger's Eye: This stone resembles the actual eye of a tiger. Similar to a tiger that crouches and waits to spring upon its prey, this stone helps improve your patience and skills to make money. It supports savings and when to spend to improve your prosperity.

10. Sunstone: This stone will support increased prosperity as well as keeping you positive in any financial condition. It also encourages you to move ahead to achieve your goals and aspiration.

Keep these crystals with you in your purse or wallet, cash drawer of your business, in your change bowl or in the wealth corner of your house, which is the furthest left corner from your front door. My personal favorite crystal for bringing in wealth and abundance is Citrine.

"Yesterday I was clever, so I wanted to change the world. Today I am wise, so I am changing myself."
- Rumi

Rock Star Beliefs

Turn the following common, limiting beliefs on their heads and unleash all that 'hidden' abundance. It's not really hidden; you're just not walking in your power. When we take an active role, heal the shame and trauma, maintain our alignment or use tools that resonate with us, we take a power position with our money. If any of these beliefs are yours or have been yours, consciously shift them to unlock your money. Be a rock star; unleash abundance.

1. You believe money is the root of all evil

Not all rich people are seedy drug dealers or have obtained their wealth by swindling other people out of their lunch money or their life savings. Money can create and support freedom, joy, creativity, adventure and many other awesome things. Try and focus on the positive impact that money can have in other people's lives. If you had lots of money, think of whom you could share it with, whom you could support and of how you could help change the world.

Abundance Unleashed:

Remember and affirm that money is a flow of energy into your life to support you, the people who you believe in and the causes that are important to you. It's a mutual exchange based on what your revenue streams are.

2. You don't bend down to pick up pennies, that's embarrassing!

"See a penny pick it up, all day long you'll have good luck."

Do you pick up the tiny shiny coin in the Costco parking lot, or do you feel embarrassed and think others might see you and think you're broke? Does fear of judgment stop you? It's an only a penny, I hear people say. Yes, exactly, it's a penny. A penny you didn't have a minute ago. Stop measuring money by what it can buy you, measure it by the joy it brings.

Abundance Unleashed:

Let the Universe know you are GRATEFUL for every little piece of good fortune you are presented with. Pick up the penny and say thank you. It's a sign of alignment and that MORE is on its way. Acknowledge it. There's more where that came from.

3. You complain about how much things cost

When you always say that things are "too expensive" or you verbally express fear around spending money, it deactivates your intentions to attract more. Love your bills; thank your money as it exchanges hands. Fear of spending money is living in scarcity – because you feel that there isn't enough money.

Abundance Unleashed:

Choose your words wisely and remember that your words activate your vibration and return to you as your reality. When you pay a bill, say, "Thank you. I love sending money to people who support my success." Don't hang out with people who use 'broke language'.

4. You don't put a dollar value on your time

Are you too nice and unable to say no to people when they ask for your help? Do you feel weird charging friends or family for your expertise? Even if it's a discounted rate, you need to value your time and place a dollar value on it. Why? Because you are worthy. It shows the Universe that every hour of the day is an opportunity to be open to the flow of money.

Abundance Unleashed:

Be sure to honor your time in all situations. You are worthy. You exist and are co-creating your abundance. Don't dishonor that.

5. You believe that winning the lottery will change your life

There's a reason why most lottery winners lose all of their winnings within the first three years… And that's because they haven't expanded their consciousness around money in order to keep it. They don't feel worthy enough and they don't understand how to get the money to start working for them. Gamblers are always playing catch up. Don't play catch up. Own your shit.

Abundance Unleashed:

Play the lottery, gamble or spend money frivolously only when you are in alignment and feel good about doing so. Have fun with your money, but stay in alignment. Gambling is an entertainment, not a job.

6. You never donate, support or give to charitable causes

There is a magical energy that is activated when you give to others and be of service to others. This is the life-blood of activating money. If you want to receive, then you first need to learn to give without expectations – yes, without expectation. Give for the sake of giving, just because you want to. Stay in alignment with your money in your giving practice – if it's not in alignment with your core values, then it's not in alignment with your money alignment statement.

Abundance Unleashed:

Choose a cause to support and give them money. Never refer to it as 'GIVING BACK'. To give back implies that you took something in the first place. You never took money; you just received it. You're just sharing it. Remove that phrase from your vocabulary.

7. You hide price tags from your partner after you've gone shopping

When people don't feel they are worthy enough to spend more money on a new dress or something that is a little over the price they usually pay, they create shame and they hide. Even if it's just a few dollars over the budget they HIDE the receipts. The other way of "hiding" the price is to say it costs less than it really did – in effect lying. This tells the Universe you don't feel worthy. This is the essence of lack.

Abundance Unleashed:

Be honest and upfront about your spending habits-even when it hurts. If the people in your life don't support your spending, they may not be in alignment with you and you may need to reconsider whom you share your life with.

8. You believe that "rich people" are different from you

Don't buy into the idea that ANYONE is separate from you. We are all human and in this together. If you've eaten a meal today, have a bed to sleep in tonight and have access to clean water YOU ARE RICH. You are so incredibly wealthy in comparison to many other people in this world that live on less than $5 a day. If you're reading this book, you're abundant already! Honour and recognize that.

Abundance Unleashed:

Be grateful for where you are in your life right now and don't wish it be any different. Enjoy the journey and remember we are all ONE.

9. You believe that money can only come from one source

The beautiful nature of being open to all possibilities means that money can flow into your life in a multitude of surprising and creative ways. You have to be open to allowing those possibilities to flow into your reality. It is not your role to know HOW it is your role to know that it is so.

Abundance can come from many different sources and it could be something you didn't actually pay for. Recognizing the "freebies" and discounts that happen in your life is acknowledging the value that is being attracted to you. Next time someone pays for your coffee – say thank you to them, but also thank the Universe. Recognition is key to bringing in more.

Abundance Unleashed:

Say yes to opportunities, events, meeting people and being out there in the world. This will let the Universe know you are open the flow of abundance from various sources. Say, "I receive gratefully!"

"Accountability breeds response – ability."
- Stephen Covey

30 Days of Money Journalling

You may recall earlier we talked about abundance journaling. I invite you to complete 30 days of journaling about money and see what comes up. Answer one question each day that prompts you to think critically, creatively and express yourself. Again, write like no one is ever going to read it. You may be surprised at what unfolds.

1. What is your first memory about money? What happened and why do you remember it?

_____
_____
_____
_____
_____
_____
_____
_____
_____
_____
_____
_____

2. So far, my experience with money has been ...

_____
_____
_____
_____
_____
_____
_____
_____
_____
_____
_____
_____
_____
_____
_____
_____

3. What did your parents say about money and did their actions back up their words? List five things you remember hearing and five things you remember about their actions.

_____
_____
_____
_____
_____
_____
_____
_____
_____
_____
_____
_____
_____
_____
_____

4. What do you believe about money?

_____
_____
_____
_____
_____
_____
_____
_____
_____
_____
_____
_____
_____
_____
_____
_____
_____

5. Finish this sentence: "My soul believes that money is…."
_____
_____
_____
_____
_____
_____
_____
_____
_____
_____
_____
_____

6. Are you comfortable with earning lots of money? What does "lots of money" mean to you?
_____
_____
_____
_____
_____
_____
_____
_____
_____
_____
_____
_____
_____
_____
_____
_____

7. If you had unlimited money, what would you buy right now?

___

8. How would you LIKE to feel about money?

___

9. Being empowered about money would mean ...
___

10. Write a letter to money, as if money were a person.
___

11. If you had to spend $1 million dollars in 24 hours, what would you do? Be specific.

___

12. What are you willing to do to work on your relationship with money?

___

13. Imagine having a conversation with your parents about money, how does that make you feel?

_____
_____
_____
_____
_____
_____
_____
_____
_____
_____
_____
_____
_____

14. Imagine having a conversation with your partner about money, how does that make you feel?

_____
_____
_____
_____
_____
_____
_____
_____
_____
_____
_____
_____
_____

15. Finish this sentence: "Being happy with money would mean…"

_____
_____
_____
_____
_____
_____
_____
_____
_____
_____
_____
_____

16. Finish this sentence: "Being creative with money would mean…"

_____
_____
_____
_____
_____
_____
_____
_____
_____
_____
_____
_____
_____
_____
_____
_____

17. Imagine you have a $100 bill in your wallet. You go to the store and spend it. When you look back in your wallet, you see that there is another $100 bill. As soon as you spend it, there is another one. How would you feel?

_____
_____
_____
_____
_____
_____
_____
_____
_____
_____
_____
_____

18. Finish this sentence: "If I could change my history with money, I would…"

_____
_____
_____
_____
_____
_____
_____
_____
_____
_____
_____
_____
_____
_____

19. What do your friends believe about money? Is this a good circle?

20. Finish this sentence: "What I wish I had done with my money is…"

21. Write a forgiveness letter to yourself for a specific money mistake.
_____
_____
_____
_____
_____
_____
_____
_____
_____
_____
_____
_____

22. What is your money goal for the next six months? Why?
_____
_____
_____
_____
_____
_____
_____
_____
_____
_____
_____
_____
_____
_____
_____

23. Finish this sentence: "When I feel abundant, I am…"

_____
_____
_____
_____
_____
_____
_____
_____
_____
_____

24. Finish this sentence: "My one special treat to myself is…"

_____
_____
_____
_____
_____
_____
_____
_____
_____
_____
_____
_____
_____
_____
_____

25. What do you believe your friends and family think about how you handle money or how much money you have?

_____
_____
_____
_____
_____
_____
_____
_____
_____
_____
_____
_____
_____
_____
_____

26. Finish this sentence: "Success with money to me means…"

_____
_____
_____
_____
_____
_____
_____
_____
_____
_____
_____
_____
_____
_____
_____
_____
_____

27. Describe a rich person.

28. Finish this sentence: "What I love about money is…"

29. What is the most outrageous thing you have ever spent money on?
_____
_____
_____
_____
_____
_____
_____
_____
_____
_____
_____
_____

30. Finish this sentence: "Money is my best friend because…"
_____
_____
_____
_____
_____
_____
_____
_____
_____
_____
_____
_____
_____
_____
_____
_____
_____

You Did It!

You uncovered your core shame story, your generational beliefs, your limiting beliefs and you rewrote your story. You learned how to be accountable to your money, how to track it and acknowledge it. What now, you're probably wondering? Keep your practice going by doing the complementary practices that you are in alignment with. Surround yourself with Money Rock Stars and rock the crap out of your abundance!

Weekly MoneyDates are momentum builders, so keep at them. Highlight your Money Alignment Statement by putting it in places where you will see it, and you will be reminded of how you want to feel, think and see money in your life. Celebrate! Seriously, you're a Rock Star!

Celebrate and announce your abundance to the world. It's not showing off, it is inspiring to others. Be a shining example of what is possible and other's will be inspired to make shifts in their own lives.

I would love to hear about your journey. Connect with me on social media! I love hearing from Money Rock Stars.

Let's keep the conversation going.

About the Author

Growing up on the West Coast of Canada, Michelle learned at an early age that money equaled hard work and sacrifice. As she watched her father and brothers work physically hard to earn money in the commercial fishing industry, she adopted that same attitude. It has to be a struggle, there has to be sacrifice – and if it doesn't feel that way, well damn well make it feel that way – so she became an over-achiever. Justifying her pay cheque by working long hours, dedicated to her job, over delivering for her pay cheque. Well, that only gets you so far. The same became true when she started her own business – those limiting beliefs kicked in and she found herself in the same position but with herself as the "boss".

It became clear to Michelle that there was a missing piece to this puzzle of money. She found herself creating the most amazing strategic financial growth plans for her clients, but often that didn't matter because their own limiting beliefs took over and they continued to struggle. This is where self-discovery kicked in for Michelle. She spent time learning about limiting beliefs, meditation, trust, intuition, spirituality, and all the practices that go alongside to support growth and abundance.

And this is where the magic happened. Michelle realized that she had a unique insight and ability to marry the masculine and feminine energy of money and support people to bring all kinds of abundance into their lives –, especially money. This felt like an incredible gift she had been given and she had a responsibility to share it with the world.

Connect with Michelle:
https://www.michellebcooper.com/
Instagram: @michellebcooper
YouTube: https://www.youtube.com/channel/UCL7bEKQMGFkkSw7rbKvzGfw

Notes

Create Your Desired Reality

Are you ready to go deeper with your money manifesting? **Confessions of a Money Rock Star** is just the beginning. Michelle offers courses and circles to continue this work.

Money Rock Star Course: moneyrockstar.ca

The Companion Journal to Confessions of a Money Rock Star...

Your MoneyDate Journal is Available on Amazon.

www.ingramcontent.com/pod-product-compliance
Lightning Source LLC
Chambersburg PA
CBHW042006150426

43194CB00003B/138